Profiles of the Presidents

JAMES
MADISON

★ ★ ★

Profiles of the Presidents

JAMES MADISON

by Andrew Santella

Content Adviser: Lee Langston-Harrison, Director of Curatorial Operations, James Madison's Montpelier, Montpelier Station, Virginia

Reading Adviser: Dr. Linda D. Labbo, Department of Reading Education, College of Education, The University of Georgia

COMPASS POINT BOOKS ✦ MINNEAPOLIS, MINNESOTA

Compass Point Books
3109 West 50th Street, #115
Minneapolis, MN 55410

Visit Compass Point Books on the Internet at *www.compasspointbooks.com*
or e-mail your request to *custserv@compasspointbooks.com*

Photographs ©: Hulton/Archive by Getty Images, cover, 3, 18, 23, 24, 25 (top), 29, 31, 32, 35, 37, 38, 40 (top), 41, 49, 54 (bottom right), 55, 56 (all), 57, 58, 59 (all); North Wind Picture Archives, 6, 7, 8, 14, 17, 21, 26, 27, 34, 36, 40 (bottom), 44, 45, 46; Belle Grove Plantation, 9, 54 (left); Lee Snider/Corbis, 11 (all); Robert Holmes/Corbis, 12; Corbis, 15; Bettmann/Corbis, 16, 39, 47 (top); National Portrait Gallery, Smithsonian Institution/Art Resource, N.Y., 19; Stock Montage, 20 (top), 33, 42, 54 (top right); Francis G. Mayer/Corbis, 20 (bottom); Joseph Sohm; Visions of America/Corbis, 22; The Newberry Library/Stock Montage, 25 (bottom); Courtesy of Montpelier, watercolor by Devin Floyd, 50.

Editors: E. Russell Primm, Emily J. Dolbear, Melissa McDaniel, and Catherine Neitge
Photo Researcher: Svetlana Zhurkina
Photo Selector: Linda S. Koutris
Designer: The Design Lab
Cartographer: XNR Productions, Inc.

Library of Congress Cataloging-in-Publication Data

Santella, Andrew.
  James Madison / by Andrew Santella.
    v. cm. — (Profiles of the presidents)
  Includes bibliographical references and index.
  Contents: Mr. Madison's war—A Virginia boyhood—Serving a new nation—A national leader—
President Madison—Preparing for war—Attack on Washington—After Madison's Presidency—
Glossary—James Madison's life at a glance—James Madison's life and times—World events—
Understanding James Madison and his Presidency.
  ISBN 0-7565-0252-7
  1. Madison, James, 1751–1836—Juvenile literature. 2. Presidents—United States—Biography—
Juvenile literature. [1. Madison, James, 1751–1836. 2. Presidents.] I. Title. II. Series.
  E342 .S27 2003
    973.5'1'092—dc21   2002003032

Table of Contents

★ ★ ★

Mr. Madison's War

★ ★ ★

People called it "Mr. Madison's War." In fact, though, James Madison had tried to avoid a war with Great Britain. For years, the British navy had been capturing American sailors at sea and forcing them to join the British navy. The United States demanded that Britain stop this practice.

Madison tried to find peaceful ways to stop the British attacks. He ended American trade with Great

The British navy, in need of sailors, took American seamen against their will.

Britain. He had U.S. representatives in Great Britain demand a halt to the attacks. Nothing worked.

As a result, on June 1, 1812, Madison sent a secret message to the U.S. Congress. Madison wrote that the United States had tried to be peaceful, but "we behold on the side of Great Britain a state of war against the United States." Madison believed the United States had no choice but to declare war on Great Britain. "Peace as we now have it is disgraceful," he wrote, "and war [would be] honorable."

◄ *James Madison*

Congress agreed. Both the House of Representatives and the Senate approved a declaration of war on Great Britain, and Madison signed it on June 18, 1812. "Mr. Madison's War," or the War of 1812, was on.

By this time, Madison had already done much to serve his country. Before he became president, he had been a leader in writing the United States Constitution. Then he guided the effort to get it approved. Later, he served as secretary of state under President Thomas Jefferson.

The War of 1812, however, was a different kind of challenge for Madison. He had to prepare his country to fight a war against Great Britain, the greatest military power in the world. The future of the young country depended on Madison's ability to rise to this new challenge. The war he never wanted would become the main event of James Madison's presidency.

In 1787, the nation's leaders, including James Madison, met in Philadelphia to draw up the Constitution.

A Virginia Boyhood

★ ★ ★

James Madison was born on March 16, 1751. He was the first son of James Madison and Nelly Conway Madison. James's father was a farmer and a leader in the local church. He also was an officer in the county **militia**. Local people called him the Colonel. As the firstborn son of his family, the Colonel had inherited land and money from his father.

◄ Colonel James Madison

He added to his growing wealth as a young man by marrying into a rich family. His wife, Nelly Conway Madison, was the daughter of a wealthy tobacco merchant. The Madisons had eleven children after young James, but only seven of them survived past early childhood.

Young James was born at the home of his mother's family, in Port Conway, Virginia. He grew up on the family plantation in Orange County, Virginia. The Madison plantation was like many other Virginia plantations of the time. It covered about 5,000 acres (2,023 hectares) and produced tobacco and grain. Farming such a large plantation required a large workforce. In Virginia at that time, slaves did the hard work on large plantations. James Madison's father owned about 100 slaves.

When James was a boy, the Colonel began building a new house on his plantation. It stood high on a hill, with a view of the beautiful Blue Ridge Mountains in the distance. The Colonel named the house Montpelier, after a town in France.

In many ways, James Madison enjoyed a typical childhood for the son of a wealthy Virginia family. Jemmy, as everyone called him, learned to ride horses.

◄ Montpelier, the Madison's second family home, as it looks today

He played with his many cousins and other relatives when they came to visit the plantation. He went to church on Sunday with his family. But Jemmy's childhood was troubled by his poor health. He was small for his age, and frail. He always seemed to be suffering from one illness or another.

◄ As the son of a wealthy Virginia planter, Madison would have attended a church like this one on Sundays.

His poor health did not stop Jemmy from reading, though. His grandmother had taught Jemmy to read and write, and it quickly became his favorite pastime. As he grew older, he became interested in learning classical languages, such as Latin and Greek.

When Jemmy turned eleven, the Colonel sent him to a plantation school to study. These small schools were

A plantation school ▾

run by teachers out of their own homes or neighboring plantations. Children from the surrounding area would come to the plantation to live and study, as they would at a boarding school. Jemmy stayed at the plantation school for five years, studying mathematics, science, Latin, Greek, and French.

When he was sixteen, Jemmy began studying with Reverend Thomas Martin. Martin was only twenty-five, and the teacher and student became friends. When their lessons were finished, they spent hours talking about politics and current events. After two years of study with Martin, Jemmy was ready for college. Martin suggested he enroll at the College of New Jersey—now called Princeton University. So in the fall of 1769, Jemmy headed north to New Jersey to begin his college education. The 300-mile (483-kilometer) trip took ten days by horseback.

At eighteen, Jemmy was older than some of his Princeton classmates. (At that time, many students began college at sixteen.) He was also one of the best students in his class. He took part in debates, even though he did not like public speaking. His talent at writing arguments often helped his side win the debates.

The College of New ▶
Jersey at Princeton,
New Jersey

Madison worked so hard at college that he was able to graduate in just two years.

When Jemmy Madison returned home, he was still unsure about his future. Then, in 1774, he was given the chance to take part in Virginia politics. He became a member of the Orange County Committee of Safety. The committee was a local group made up of people who disliked the way Great Britain was treating its American **colonies.** Such groups had sprung up throughout the

British colonies. On the local level, they directed the struggle against Great Britain. As a member of the Committee of Safety, Madison was in the middle of the growing conflict between Great Britain and the colonies. It was his first experience in politics—James Madison had found his calling.

▼ Increasingly, conflicts arose between colonial Americans and the British.

Serving a New Nation

★ ★ ★

When the colonies declared their independence from Great Britain in 1776, Madison became even more involved in politics. That year, Virginia held a **convention** to write a new state **constitution,** and Madison was chosen to attend. There he met Thomas Jefferson. The

James Madison and Thomas Jefferson were good friends through their entire lives.

two men worked together to make sure the new state constitution protected religious freedom. They remained close friends for the rest of their lives.

In 1778, Madison was appointed to the Virginia Council

of State. This council advised the governor and helped run the state government during the Revolutionary War (1775–1783). In 1780, Virginians elected Madison to the Continental Congress in Philadelphia, Pennsylvania.

The Continental Congress was made up of representatives from all the American states. Many of the greatest and most famous men in the United States were in the Continental Congress. Madison was only twenty-nine,

The old state house of Philadelphia, now Independence Hall, was the site for many important meetings of the founding fathers.

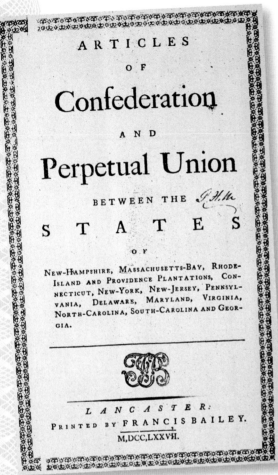

ARTICLES

OF

Confederation

AND

Perpetual Union

BETWEEN THE *J.H.M*

S T A T E S

OF

NEW-HAMPSHIRE, MASSACHUSETTS-BAY, RHODE-ISLAND AND PROVIDENCE PLANTATIONS, CONNECTICUT, NEW-YORK, NEW-JERSEY, PENNSYLVANIA, DELAWARE, MARYLAND, VIRGINIA, NORTH-CAROLINA, SOUTH-CAROLINA AND GEORGIA.

L A N C A S T E R:
PRINTED BY F R A N C I S B A I L E Y.
M,DCC,LXXVII.

The Articles of Confederation were in effect from 1781 to 1788.

but he made a name for himself as one of the brightest and hardest-working members of the Congress.

Madison's three years in Congress were frustrating, however. At the time, the thirteen former colonies were loosely joined under the **Articles of Confederation.** Under this document, the national government was weak and disorganized. For example, Congress lacked the power to tax citizens. Instead, it relied on the states for funds. The nation had no president to provide leadership, and there was no national court system. Madison and others became convinced that the United States needed a new system of government.

In 1784, Madison was elected to the Virginia House of Delegates, part of Virginia's state **legislature.** As a member of the Virginia legislature, Madison worked to prevent the government from using tax money to teach Christianity. In debates with the great Virginia statesman Patrick Henry, Madison spoke out against government support of religious beliefs.

Madison also led in the reshaping of the national government of the United States. Thanks partly to his efforts, each state sent **delegates** to a Constitutional Convention that began in Philadelphia on May 14, 1787.

▼ *Patrick Henry famously declared "Give me liberty or give me death!"*

Madison was elected to be one of Virginia's delegates. He quickly emerged as a leader in the movement to create a stronger central government. He overcame his shyness and led the debate at the convention. He helped create what came to be called the Virginia Plan. It called for a national legislature, a chief executive (the president), and

Alexander Hamilton ▶

John Jay ▶

independent courts, including a Supreme Court. All of these were included in the Constitution.

The new Constitution was signed on September 17, 1787, but nine of the thirteen states had to approve the document before it would take effect. All over the United States, people argued for and against the Constitution. Some feared that giving greater power to the central government would cost ordinary people their freedom. Madison and two well-known New Yorkers—lawyer Alexander Hamilton and judge John Jay—published a series of essays in newspapers in support of the new Constitution. They came to be called *The Federalist.* Madison wrote twenty-nine of the eighty-five essays. He argued that a strong government was the best way to protect people's freedom. He also explained how each branch of government would keep the other branches from gaining too much power. This kind of government came to be called the system of checks and balances.

Virginia and eight other states approved the Constitution in June 1788. The Constitution then became the guiding document of the new United States government. Madison played such a key role in creating and defending the document that he became known as the Father of the Constitution.

Madison won election to the newly formed House of Representatives in 1789. There he continued to work to

▲ *An early copy of*
The Federalist

The U.S. Constitution

◄ *The Bill of Rights*

improve the Constitution. He proposed the first ten amendments, or changes, to the Constitution. These became known as the Bill of Rights. These ten amendments were added because some people believed that the rights and freedoms of individuals were not protected by the Constitution. The Bill of Rights spelled out the rights that every American should enjoy, including freedom of speech, freedom of religion, and the right to a fair trial.

The first presidential cabinet, including Thomas Jefferson and Alexander Hamilton

As a member of Congress, Madison agreed with most of the policies of George Washington, the first president. But Madison disagreed with the economic policies of Alexander Hamilton, who had become Washington's secretary of the treasury. Madison believed that Hamilton's policies favored banks and wealthy northerners over the planters of the southern states. This disagreement helped create the first American political parties. Madison and Thomas Jefferson became leaders of the Democratic-Republican Party, sometimes called simply the Republicans. Hamilton became the leader of the Federalist Party.

During this period, Madison's personal life was changing. On September 15, 1794, he married Dolley Payne Todd. She was a widow from Philadelphia with a son who was almost three years old. Madison raised the boy, John Payne Todd, as his own.

In 1797, Madison retired from Congress and returned to Virginia with Dolley. After only a year, he was drawn into politics again. In 1798, Federalists in Congress passed a series of laws called the Alien and Sedition Acts. Aliens are people born in another country. These laws made it a crime to criticize the government, and gave the president the power to throw aliens out of the country. Madison was

▲ Dolley Madison

▲ John Payne Todd

Map of the U.S. showing the Louisiana Purchase

enraged by the Alien and Sedition Acts. He believed they ignored the freedoms protected by the Bill of Rights. He wrote a protest called the Virginia Resolutions that declared the acts **unconstitutional.** The Virginia Resolutions were adopted by the Virginia state legislature.

In 1800, Madison's friend Thomas Jefferson won the presidential election. He asked Madison to be his secretary of state—the person responsible for the U.S. government's relations with other countries. Probably the greatest achievement of Madison's term was buying Louisiana from

France in 1803. The Louisiana Purchase added 827,987 square miles (2,144,476 square kilometers) of territory to the United States, doubling the nation's size.

Some of Madison's other efforts were not so successful, however. At that time, Great Britain and France were at war, and both countries attacked American ships at sea. In addition, the British captured American sailors and forced them to join the British navy. Jefferson and Madison looked for a way to punish the British and French without going to war. They supported the **Embargo** Act of 1807, which stopped Americans from sending **exports** to Europe. The embargo turned out to be a disaster for the United States, however. It did little to stop the attacks by Great Britain and France, but it hurt American merchants, who had fewer markets for their goods because of the embargo. There seemed to be no easy way to solve the problem. In the years ahead, however, Madison would keep searching for an answer.

▼ *The British navy was considered the best in the world.*

President Madison

★　★　★

After completing two terms as president, Thomas Jefferson decided not to run for a third term. Instead, he urged Madison to run.

With Jefferson's support, Madison became the choice of the Democratic-Republican Party. His opponent in the 1808 election was Federalist Charles C. Pinckney of South Carolina. The Federalists were sure they could defeat Madison. Many New Englanders disliked Madison and blamed him for the economic distress caused by the Embargo Act. Federalists said that Madison's policies were ruining American business. They also made fun of his size and his shyness.

Their attacks failed. Madison won the election of 1808 by a wide margin and became the fourth president of the United States. He began his presidency with a historic party. After Madison's **inauguration** on March

4, 1809, Dolley Madison hosted a fancy ball, or celebration. That inaugural ball became a tradition followed by most new presidents.

The party on Inauguration Night was the first of many Dolley would host at the President's House. (The President's House was not officially called the White

◄ *Dolley Madison hosted many parties at the President's House.*

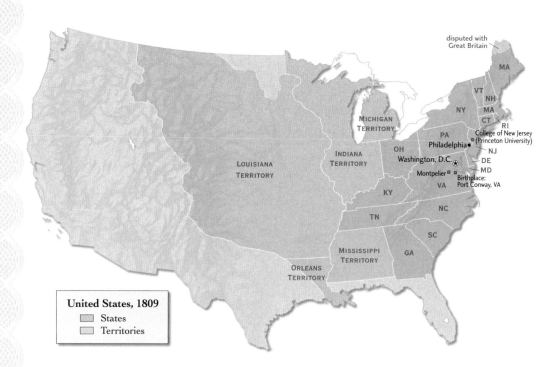

disputed with
Great Britain

MA

VT
NH
NY MA
CT
RI
College of New Jersey
(Princeton University)
PA
Philadelphia
NJ
MICHIGAN
TERRITORY
OH DE
Washington, D.C. MD
INDIANA
TERRITORY
Montpelier
Birthplace:
Port Conway, VA
LOUISIANA
TERRITORY
VA
KY
NC
TN
SC
MISSISSIPPI
TERRITORY GA
ORLEANS
TERRITORY

United States, 1809
States
Territories

House until President Theodore Roosevelt authorized
that title in 1901.) Dolley Madison became famous for
her fancy parties and her fashionable clothes. She redec-
orated the President's House and hung portraits of the
first three presidents.

Her husband did not get off to such a good start as
president, though. Just before Madison became president, Congress had replaced the Embargo Act. The new
act allowed Americans to trade with all other countries
except Great Britain and France. Both Great Britain and
France told Madison that they would stop attacking

◄ *The first Bank of the United States in Philadelphia*

American ships, but only if the United States would declare war on the other country. Madison refused to be drawn into that war, however. Later, France agreed to stop attacking American ships, but Great Britain continued to attack American ships and capture American sailors.

Madison also came into conflict with members of his own Democratic-Republican Party in Congress. In 1811, Congress had to decide whether to renew the **charter** of the Bank of the United States. The government put the money it collected through taxes in that bank. Its charter was due to end in 1812, and only

Congress could renew it. Most Democratic-Republicans in Congress disliked the bank because they believed it gave the central government too much power. But Madison favored the bank. He thought it was an important source of money for the government during emergencies. Because Madison did not want to anger members of his own party in Congress, however, he allowed the bank's charter to end.

Madison faced other problems, too. Some of the government officials he had appointed were not doing their jobs well. His first secretary of state, Robert Smith, was so disloyal that he made fun of Madison behind his back. In 1811, Madison fired Smith and replaced him with James Monroe, a fellow Virginian and longtime friend.

Robert Smith ▲

Preparing for War

★ ★ ★

By 1811, an increasing number of Americans were calling for war with Great Britain. That year, American Indians led by Tecumseh, the Shawnee chief, attacked settlements in Indiana Territory, Kentucky, and other states. Many Americans believed that Great Britain was encouraging the Indians to attack. Young Democratic-Republican congressmen from southern and western states were demanding war with Great Britain. Led by Henry

▲ *Tecumseh*

Henry Clay ▲

Clay of Kentucky and John C. Calhoun of South Carolina, these congressmen came to be called War Hawks. They wanted to declare war on Great Britain, invade Canada, and expand the United States across all of North America.

Madison realized that the United States was not prepared for war with Great Britain. He also knew that many of the people in New England and New York were against war and that he might need their votes in the presidential election of 1812. Still, he insisted that Great Britain stop its attacks on American ships. Messages went back and forth between Madison and British leaders. At that time, it took weeks for a message to make its way across the Atlantic Ocean by ship. In

August 1812, the
British govern-
ment finally sent
word to Madison
that it was will-
ing to stop its
attacks on Amer-
ican ships. It
came too late,
however. Before
the message
arrived, Madison
had asked
Congress to

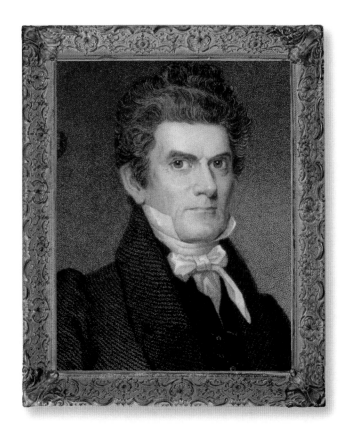

▲ *John C. Calhoun*

declare war on Great Britain. The War of 1812 had
already begun.

Even as he armed America for war, Madison had to
prepare for another struggle. In 1812, he ran for a second term as president. The election of 1812 was the
first presidential election in American history that took
place while the nation was at war. As in 1808, Madison
ran with the support of the Democratic-Republican
Party. Madison ran against De Witt Clinton, the mayor

A sea battle ▶
during the
War of 1812

of New York. Clinton had the support of Federalists who were against the war with Great Britain. He also had the support of some Democratic-Republicans who believed that Madison had not been a good president.

▲ *De Witt Clinton*

Clinton won 89 electoral votes—all from New England and northern states. Madison won 128 electoral votes, mostly from southern states, but also from Pennsylvania, Ohio, and Vermont. It was a narrow victory for Madison, but it was enough to give him a second term as president.

Of course, the most pressing challenge of Madison's second term was the war. The British military forces were considered to be the most powerful in the world. At that time, the U. S. Army was poorly trained and badly led. The American war effort was also held back by Federalists in Congress who fought any attempts to raise taxes to pay for the war.

The war started badly for the United States. American forces trying to invade British-controlled Canada were beaten at Detroit and at Niagara Falls. Some Federalists in New England states even talked of leaving the Union because the war was hurting business in New England.

In the summer of 1813, Madison became seriously ill with a fever. He soon recovered, and the American war effort improved, too. In 1813, an American force invaded Canada. The soldiers reached Toronto, where they burned several government buildings. Then, an American naval force under Commodore Oliver Hazard Perry defeated British ships on Lake Erie. Finally, an

James Madison, the ▲ fourth U.S. president

American general William Hull surrenders to the British at Detroit.

Alexander I, Czar ▲
of Russia

Albert Gallatin ▼

American army defeated a British and Indian force at the Battle of the Thames River in Ontario, Canada.

Madison was heartened by the victories but he was also ready to seek an end to the war. Late in 1813, Czar Alexander, Russia's leader, offered to arrange peace between the United States and Great Britain. The peace talks began in August 1814, in the Belgian city of Ghent. Madison asked Secretary of the Treasury Albert Gallatin to lead the American team there. Madison's stepson, John Payne Todd, served as Gallatin's aide during the talks.

Even as the peace talks began, the British launched
a new assault against the United States. British ships
attacked ports all along the Atlantic coast. Then British
troops sailed up Chesapeake Bay, toward Washington,
D.C. Madison ordered Secretary of War John Armstrong
to protect Washington, but Armstrong believed that the
British were headed for Baltimore. When the British

▾ *The British attack
Washington, D.C.,
in August 1814*

Dolley Madison ▶
saved important
documents
before leaving
the President's
House.

began marching on Washington, American troops were unable to stop them.

Madison joined American troops outside Washington at Bladensburg, Maryland. He told Dolley to leave Washington and arranged to meet her at a safe place in Virginia. Dolley insisted on staying in the President's House as long as possible. Finally, she gathered some official documents and a portrait of George Washington and fled the city. Just hours later, British troops marched into Washington. They set the President's House and other government buildings on fire. The President's House burned all night, until a heavy rain put out the flames. Then the British left Washington to continue their invasion.

The Madisons returned to Washington three days after the attack. Most people blamed Secretary of War John Armstrong for the American defeat. He left his job, and Madison appointed James Monroe to take his place. Dolley helped organize **volunteers** to clean up burned buildings. Work was not completed on the President's House until 1817, so the Madisons lived elsewhere.

British forces had little success after taking Washington. An American victory at Fort McHenry in Baltimore

The Battle
of New
Orleans

Harbor on September 13 inspired Francis Scott Key to write "The Star-Spangled Banner." Another British force was stopped on January 8, 1815, at the Battle of New Orleans. This turned out to be the last battle of the War of 1812. Ten days later, news arrived from Belgium that U.S. and British representatives had signed a peace treaty

▲ *Though the President's House and the Capitol burned, most of Washington was saved by a rainstorm.*

★

Francis Scott Key, ▲
author of "The Star-
Spangled Banner"

ending the war. The Treaty of Ghent had been signed on December 24, 1814—about two weeks before the Battle of New Orleans. News of the treaty did not make its way across the Atlantic Ocean until after the battle.

The treaty called for a return to the conditions that existed before the war. Great Britain gave up the territory it had captured in the war and also agreed to stop its attacks on American ships and sailors. The peace treaty was a disaster for the Federalist Party, which had been against the war. Now that the war was over, the Federalists looked unwise and even disloyal. The Federalist Party was never again a major force in American politics. The United States entered a period marked by less intense political disagreement. During the following years, this period came to be called "The Era of Good Feeling."

In his final months as president, Madison signed bills that rechartered the Bank of the United States. In addition, he helped create a fund for disabled war veterans. He had also hoped to establish a national university in Washington, D.C., but Congress rejected his plan.

▲ *James Madison*

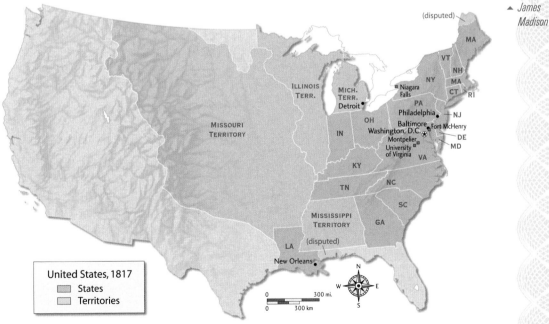

(disputed)

MA
VT
NH
NY   MA
■ Niagara   CT   RI
Falls
ILLINOIS   PA
TERR.   MICH.   Philadelphia ● ┤ NJ
TERR.   Baltimore ● Fort McHenry
Detroit ●   Washington, D.C. ⊛   ● DE
OH   Montpelier ■   MD
MISSOURI   IN   University ■
TERRITORY   of Virginia   VA
KY
TN   NC
SC
MISSISSIPPI   GA
TERRITORY
LA   (disputed)
New Orleans ●

N
W ⊕ E
S

United States, 1817
☐ States
☐ Territories

0   300 mi.
0   300 km

After Madison's Presidency

★   ★   ★

Madison hoped that James Monroe would follow him as president. With Madison's support, Monroe won the election of 1816. Like Madison, Monroe was a Virginian. In fact, Monroe was the fourth of the first five presidents to come from Virginia.

Madison retired to Montpelier to run his plantation, but he was not finished with public service. In 1826, Madison, already a member of the Board of Trustees at the University of Virginia, became the university's rector. In 1829, he served as a delegate to the convention that changed Virginia's state constitution. He also helped found the American Colonization Society, a group that wanted to establish a colony in Africa for freed slaves.

James Madison died at Montpelier on June 28, 1836. After his death, Dolley returned to Washington. There, her charm and tact made her a favorite guest at fashionable parties. She died on July 12, 1849.

Madison is known to most Americans as the Father of the Constitution. His achievements as president are less well known, but they are also important. He led the United States through a difficult war and earned the respect of other nations. Mr. Madison's War showed the world that

▼ The University of Virginia in 1830

the United States would protect its citizens. For the second time, the United States had stood up to the mighty British military. Many people saw Mr. Madison's War as a second successful War for Independence.

James Madison's ▶
tombstone

GLOSSARY

★ ★ ★

Articles of Confederation—the first constitution of the United States. It gave the central government much less power than the present Constitution does.

charter—a government order giving a company the right to do business

colonies—territories settled by people from another country and ruled by that country

constitution—a document stating the basic rules of a government

convention—a meeting held for a special purpose

delegates—people who represent a larger group of people at a meeting

embargo—a government order that stops trade

exports—things made or grown in one country and sold in another country

inauguration—a president's swearing-in ceremony

legislature—the part of government that makes or changes laws

militia—an army of part-time soldiers

unconstitutional—not agreeing with the U.S. Constitution

volunteers—people who offer to do a job, usually without pay

JAMES MADISON'S LIFE AT A GLANCE

★ ★ ★

PERSONAL

Nickname:	Father of the Constitution
Born:	March 16, 1751
Birthplace:	Port Conway, Virginia
Father's name:	James Madison
Mother's name:	Nelly Conway Madison
Education:	Graduated in 1771 from the College of New Jersey (now Princeton University)
Wife's name:	Dolley Payne Todd Madison
Married:	September 15, 1794
Children:	None
Died:	June 28, 1836, at Montpelier
Buried:	Montpelier Estate, Orange County, Virginia

PUBLIC

Occupation before presidency:	Planter, lawyer
Occupation after presidency:	Planter, statesman
Military service:	Colonel in the Orange County Militia
Other government positions:	Orange County Committee of Safety; Governor's Council in Virginia; member of the Continental Congress; member of the Constitutional Convention; representative for Virginia in the U.S. House of Representatives; secretary of state
Political party:	Democratic-Republican
Vice presidents:	George Clinton (1809–1812), Elbridge Gerry (1813–1814)
Dates in office:	March 4, 1809–March 3, 1817
Presidential opponents:	Charles C. Pinckney (Federalist), 1808; De Witt Clinton (Federalist), 1812
Number of votes (Electoral College):	(122 of 176), 1808; (128 of 218), 1812
Writings:	Constitution of the United States of America, *The Federalist*

★

James Madison's Cabinet

Secretary of state:
Robert Smith (1809–1811)
James Monroe (1811–1817)

Secretary of the treasury:
Albert Gallatin (1809–1814)
George W. Campbell (1814)
Alexander J. Dallas (1814–1816)
William H. Crawford (1816–1817)

Secretary of war:
William Eustis (1809–1812)
John Armstrong (1813–1814)
James Monroe (1814–1815)
William H. Crawford (1815–1816)

Attorney general:
Caesar A. Rodney (1809–1811)
William Pinkney (1811–1814)
Richard Rush (1814–1817)

Secretary of the navy:
Paul Hamilton (1809–1812)
William Jones (1813–1814)
Benjamin W. Crowninshield (1814–1817)

JAMES MADISON'S LIFE AND TIMES

★ ★ ★

MADISON'S LIFE

1751 Madison is born on March 16 in Port Conway, Virginia, to James (below) and Nelly Madison

WORLD EVENTS

1752 Benjamin Franklin performs his famous kite experiment (below)

1759 The British Museum opens in London

1762 Catherine the Great becomes empress of Russia and rules for thirty-four years

1760

MADISON'S LIFE

Attends the College of New Jersey (now Princeton University) — 1769–1771

Becomes a colonel in the Orange County militia — 1775

Is elected a delegate to the Virginia Constitutional Convention — 1776

Serves as a Virginia delegate to the Continental Congress — 1780

1770

1780

WORLD EVENTS

1769   British explorer Captain James Cook reaches New Zealand

1770   Five die in a street clash known as the Boston Massacre (below)

1777   Vermont is the first former colony to ban slavery

1779   Jan Ingenhousz of the Netherlands discovers that plants release oxygen when exposed to sunlight

1783   American author Washington Irving is born

MADISON'S LIFE

Serves as a Virginia delegate to the Constitutional Convention	1787
Along with Alexander Hamilton and John Jay, publishes essays in support of the new Constitution. These become known as *The Federalist*.	1787–1788
Is elected to the House of Representatives	1789
Sponsors the Bill of Rights	
Helps Thomas Jefferson create the Democratic-Republican Party	

WORLD EVENTS

1790

1791	Austrian composer Wolfgang Amadeus Mozart (above) dies
1792	The dollar currency is introduced to America

September 15, marries Dolley Payne Todd (left)	1794
Returns to Montpelier	1797

MADISON'S LIFE

Serves in Virginia General Assembly	1799
Serves as secretary of state under Thomas Jefferson	1801–1809

1800

al Election Results:	Popular Votes	Electoral Votes
James Madison	N/A	122
Charles C. Pinckney		47
George Clinton		6
Vote Not Cast		1
James Madison		128
De Witt Clinton		89
Vote Not Cast		1

Reopens trade with France and Great Britain	1810

1810

WORLD EVENTS

1799	Napoléon Bonaparte takes control of France
	The Rosetta stone, which was the key to understanding Egyptian hieroglyphics, is found near Rosetta, Egypt
1801	Ultraviolet radiation is discovered

1807	Robert Fulton's *Clermont* is the first reliable steamship to travel between New York City and Albany
1809	American poet and short-story writer Edgar Allen Poe is born in Boston
1810	Bernardo O'Higgins leads Chile in its fight for independence from Spain

MADISON'S LIFE		WORLD EVENTS	
June 18, the United States declares war on Great Britain, which has been capturing American sailors and forcing them into the British navy. The War of 1812 begins.	1812	1812–1814	The United States and Britain fight the War of 1812 (below)

MADISON'S LIFE		WORLD EVENTS	
April 27, U.S. troops capture York (now Toronto), Ontario, Canada	1813		
October 5, Shawnee chief Tecumseh dies at the Battle of the Thames River			
August 24, British troops invade Washington, D.C., burning the Capitol and the President's House	1814	1814–1815	European states meet in Vienna, Austria, to redraw national borders after the conclusion of the Napoléonic Wars
December 24, the Treaty of Ghent is signed, ending the War of 1812			
January 8, General Andrew Jackson wins the Battle of New Orleans, not knowing the war is over	1815		
Retires to Montpelier	1817		

MADISON'S LIFE

WORLD EVENTS

1820

1820   Susan B. Anthony, a leader of the American woman suffrage movement, is born

1821   Central American countries gain independence from Spain

1823   Mexico becomes a republic

Becomes rector of the University of Virginia (above)   1826

1826   The first photograph is taken by Joseph Niépce, a French physicist

Serves as a delegate to the Virginia Constitutional Convention   1829

1830

1829   The first practical sewing machine is invented by French tailor Barthélemy Thimonnier (above)

1833   Great Britain abolishes slavery

June 28, dies at Montpelier   1836

1836   Texans defeat Mexican troops at San Jacinto after a deadly battle at the Alamo

UNDERSTANDING JAMES MADISON AND HIS PRESIDENCY

★ ★ ★

IN THE LIBRARY

Clinton, Susan. *James Madison*. Chicago: Childrens Press, 1986.

Flanagan, Alice K. *Dolley Payne Todd Madison*.
Danbury, Conn.: Children's Press, 1997.

Gaines, Ann Graham. *James Madison: Our Fourth President*.
Chanhassen, Minn.: The Child's World, 2002.

Kelley, Brent P. *James Madison: Father of the Constitution*.
Broomall, Pa.: Chelsea House Publishers, 2000.

Malone, Mary. *James Madison*. Springfield, N.J.: Enslow Publishers, 1997.

ON THE WEB

For more information on *James Madison,* use FactHound
to track down Web sites related to this book.

1. Go to *www.facthound.com*
2. Type in this book ID: 0756502527
3. Click on the *Fetch It* button.

Your trusty FactHound will fetch the best Web sites for you!

JAMES MADISON HISTORIC SITES
ACROSS THE COUNTRY

The James Madison Museum
129 Caroline Street
Orange, VA 22960-1532
540/672-1776
To learn more about Madison,
operated by the James Madison
Memorial Foundation

James Madison's Montpelier
11407 Constitution Highway
Montpelier Station, VA 22957
540/672-2728
To see the home of three
generations of James Madison's
family, and visit Madison's grave

Octagon House
1799 New York Avenue, N.W.
Washington, DC 20006
202/638-3105
To tour the house used as the
Executive Mansion by Madison in
1814 after the President's House
was burned by the British

THE U.S. PRESIDENTS
(Years in Office)

★   ★   ★

1. **George Washington**
   (March 4, 1789–March 3, 1797)
2. **John Adams**
   (March 4, 1797–March 3, 1801)
3. **Thomas Jefferson**
   (March 4, 1801–March 3, 1809)
4. James Madison
   (March 4, 1809–March 3, 1817)
5. **James Monroe**
   (March 4, 1817–March 3, 1825)
6. **John Quincy Adams**
   (March 4, 1825–March 3, 1829)
7. **Andrew Jackson**
   (March 4, 1829–March 3, 1837)
8. **Martin Van Buren**
   (March 4, 1837–March 3, 1841)
9. **William Henry Harrison**
   (March 6, 1841–April 4, 1841)
10. **John Tyler**
    (April 6, 1841–March 3, 1845)
11. **James K. Polk**
    (March 4, 1845–March 3, 1849)
12. **Zachary Taylor**
    (March 5, 1849–July 9, 1850)
13. **Millard Fillmore**
    (July 10, 1850–March 3, 1853)
14. **Franklin Pierce**
    (March 4, 1853–March 3, 1857)
15. **James Buchanan**
    (March 4, 1857–March 3, 1861)
16. **Abraham Lincoln**
    (March 4, 1861–April 15, 1865)
17. **Andrew Johnson**
    (April 15, 1865–March 3, 1869)

18. **Ulysses S. Grant**
    (March 4, 1869–March 3, 1877)
19. **Rutherford B. Hayes**
    (March 4, 1877–March 3, 1881)
20. **James Garfield**
    (March 4, 1881–Sept 19, 1881)
21. **Chester Arthur**
    (Sept 20, 1881–March 3, 1885)
22. **Grover Cleveland**
    (March 4, 1885–March 3, 1889)
23. **Benjamin Harrison**
    (March 4, 1889–March 3, 1893)
24. **Grover Cleveland**
    (March 4, 1893–March 3, 1897)
25. **William McKinley**
    (March 4, 1897–
    September 14, 1901)
26. **Theodore Roosevelt**
    (September 14, 1901–
    March 3, 1909)
27. **William Howard Taft**
    (March 4, 1909–March 3, 1913)
28. **Woodrow Wilson**
    (March 4, 1913–March 3, 1921)
29. **Warren G. Harding**
    (March 4, 1921–August 2, 1923)
30. **Calvin Coolidge**
    (August 3, 1923–March 3, 1929)
31. **Herbert Hoover**
    (March 4, 1929–March 3, 1933)
32. **Franklin D. Roosevelt**
    (March 4, 1933–April 12, 1945)

33. **Harry S. Truman**
    (April 12, 1945–
    January 20, 1953)
34. **Dwight D. Eisenhower**
    (January 20, 1953–
    January 20, 1961)
35. **John F. Kennedy**
    (January 20, 1961–
    November 22, 1963)
36. **Lyndon B. Johnson**
    (November 22, 1963–
    January 20, 1969)
37. **Richard M. Nixon**
    (January 20, 1969–
    August 9, 1974)
38. **Gerald R. Ford**
    (August 9, 1974–
    January 20, 1977)
39. **James Earl Carter**
    (January 20, 1977–
    January 20, 1981)
40. **Ronald Reagan**
    (January 20, 1981–
    January 20, 1989)
41. **George H. W. Bush**
    (January 20, 1989–
    January 20, 1993)
42. **William Jefferson Clinton**
    (January 20, 1993–
    January 20, 2001)
43. **George W. Bush**
    (January 20, 2001–)

INDEX

★ ★ ★

ABOUT THE AUTHOR

Andrew Santella is a writer living in Cary, Illinois. He contributes to a wide range of publications, including *Gentlemen's Quarterly,* the *New York Times Magazine,* and *Commonweal.* He has written several books for children on the history of America.